TRIVIA TRACKDOWN

CHALLENGING QUESTIONS TO SHARPEN RESEARCH SKILLS
Grades 4 – 6

Written by Linda Schwartz
Illustrated by Beverly Armstrong

Social Studies & Famous People

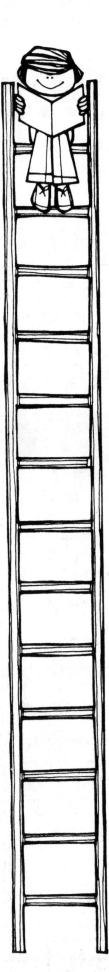

The Learning Works

Edited by Sherri M. Butterfield

The purchase of this book entitles the individual teacher to reproduce copies for use in the classroom.

The reproduction of any part for an entire school or school system or for commercial use is strictly prohibited.

No form of this work may be reproduced or transmitted or recorded without written permission from the publisher.

Trivia Trackdown
Social Studies & Famous People

Trivia Trackdown is a series of books in which challenging and unusual questions are used to stimulate thinking and to sharpen research skills. These books are divided into two sections, each related to a single area of the curriculum. In each section, there are sets of questions covering a variety of topics. These questions vary in difficulty and are based on facts found in almanacs, atlases, dictionaries, encyclopedias, world record books, and other similar reference materials. The facts have been especially selected to interest students in grades four through six. In addition to trivia, some of these research questions deal with important facts that should also be fun to track down.

You can use the question pages in this book in any or all of the following ways:

1. Have individual students select single pages and see how quickly they can find and write the answers to all ten questions. Encourage use of classroom and library reference materials.

2. Have students work in pairs to complete one sheet or all of the sheets in a section.

3. Make **Trivia Trackdown** a team effort. Suggest that groups of three or more students compete against other groups of the same size to see who can find the answers first.

4. Allow your class to challenge another class of the same grade level to a **Trivia Trackdown** contest. Evaluate answers on the basis of accuracy, completeness, and speed, and recognize the Topnotch Trivia Trackers.

5. Use selected pages as homework and encourage family participation in completing them.

6. Color, mount, and laminate at least one copy of each page. Place these pages in a learning center with appropriate reference materials. Encourage students to explore the center during their free time and to complete question pages for extra credit or just for fun.

7. Have students compile their own booklets of trivia questions and answers.

8. Instead of using **Trivia Trackdown** pages as written exercises, hold a Trivia Bee. Ask questions aloud of individual students to find a class champion.

9. Hold a Trivia Team Challenge. Divide the class into two or three groups. Ask questions aloud and keep score. At the end of a day, a week, or a month, reward the winning team.

Other Books Available in This Series

Animals & Science

Contents

Name _____

Ancient Greece

1. The Greeks of long ago believed that the highest mountain in their country was the home of a group of gods and goddesses. Name this mountain. _____

2. Who was the Greek god of the sea? _____

3. In what year were the Olympic Games first held? _____

4. A footrace was the first recorded Olympic event. Who won this race? _____

5. Who is generally thought to have been the greatest hero of the ancient Olympic Games?

    _____

6. Which Greek historian is called the "Father of History"? _____

7. One famous place in Athens is the Acropolis. It is a low, broad hill on which the ancient Greeks erected statues, monuments, temples, and a theater. What was the Acropolis originally used as? _____

8. Greek architects invented three orders of architecture. Name them. _____

    _____

9. Name the Greek architect who designed the Parthenon. _____

10. Of what material was the entire Parthenon constructed? _____

Name _____

Geography

1. Name the world's largest desert. _____

2. Which is the largest and most populous continent in the world? _____

3. Which is the world's largest and deepest ocean? _____

4. The island of Tasmania is part of which country? _____

5. Name the largest of the four Scandinavian countries. _____

6. Chad, Ghana, and the Ivory Coast are all found on which continent? _____

7. What is the highest point in North America? _____

8. Europe is not really a separate continent. Instead, it is a large peninsula that is joined on the east to another continent. Name this other continent. _____

9. The Seine River flows through which European country? _____

10. Which country is the second largest in the world? _____

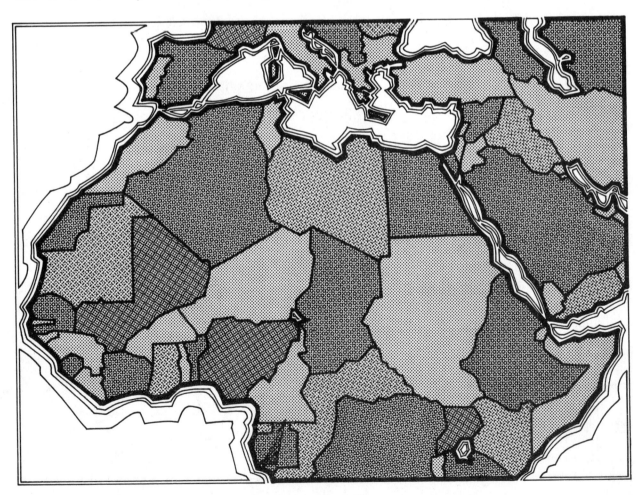

Name _____

Government

1. Who was the first woman appointed to serve as a justice of the United States Supreme Court?

   _____

2. What was President Gerald Ford's original name?_____

3. Which city was the site of the Western White House during the Nixon administration?

   _____

4. Who became president after the assassination of John Kennedy? _____

5. What did the initial in former Vice-President Hubert H. Humphrey's name stand for?

   _____

6. Who was the first chief justice of the United States Supreme Court? _____

7. Which woman was chosen to be prime minister of Israel at the age of seventy? ____

   _____

8. What is the title of the official song of the president of the United States? _____

   _____

9. Who was the first woman to hold a United States cabinet post? _____

10. Which president had a sign on his desk that read, "The buck stops here"? _____

   _____

Name _____

Maps

1. A person who draws maps is sometimes called a mapmaker. By what other name is such a person known?_____

2. What is a book of maps called? _____

3. What name is used for the explanation on a map of the symbols and scale used in drawing that map? _____

4. What mark is used to indicate the height of a spot above sea level? _____

5. What is the starting point for numbering parallels on a map? _____

6. Distance north or south of the equator measured in degrees is called what? _____

7. What kind of map shows the shape of the ground by means of shading or modeling?

_____

8. What kind of map shows natural features, such as mountains and rivers? _____

9. What kind of map shows man-made features, such as capital cities and the boundaries of states and countries? _____

10. What name is given to a map that shows seas and coastlines and is intended for use primarily by navigators? _____

Name _____

National Parks and Monuments

1. Yellowstone National Park is located in the northwest corner of which state? _____

2. The white, powdery substance in New Mexico's White Sands National Monument is not really sand. What is it? _____

3. El Capitan, Glacier Point, and Half Dome are popular landmarks in which national park?

    _____

4. In which state is Zion National Park? _____

5. What 13,680-foot volcano is located in Hawaii Volcanoes National Park? _____

6. What major river created the Grand Canyon and flows through Grand Canyon National Park? _____

7. Jackson Hole is a lush, green valley in which national park? _____

8. Joshua Tree National Monument in Arizona was named for the Joshua Tree, which is a rare, forty-foot member of which plant family? _____

9. The world's largest natural bridge is located on the Utah-Arizona border, spans 278 feet, rises 309 feet above the creek that carved it, and has been declared a national monument. What is the name of this bridge? _____

10. The largest living thing on earth is a sequoia tree found in California's Sequoia National Park. What is the name of this remarkable tree? _____

Name _____

Places of Interest

1. What was Hoover Dam on the Colorado River originally called? _____

2. What is the maximum number of names that can be chosen at one election to be honored in New York's Hall of Fame?_____

3. What is the name of the bell in the clock tower of the House of Parliament in London?

   _____

4. For what major event was the Eiffel Tower designed? _____

5. Where is the Tomb of the Unknown Soldier? _____

6. What is the name of the famous geyser in Yellowstone National Park that erupts on the average of once every 64.5 minutes? _____

7. Where was the first oil well in the United States drilled?_____

8. What is the name of the island in New York Harbor on which the Statue of Liberty stands?

   _____

9. Where is the Astrodome? _____

10. The faces of which four presidents are carved in the side of Mount Rushmore? _____

    _____

Name _____

Social Studies Potpourri

1. What was the real name of Johnny Appleseed, the man who planted apple seeds throughout the Ohio Valley? _____

2. Who designed, built, and flew an enormous wooden airplane called the *Spruce Goose?*

   _____

3. Name the first man in space. _____

4. What is the first word of the United States Constitution? _____

5. What was the medieval name for China popularized by Marco Polo? _____

6. Which country sold Alaska to the United States in 1867 for $7,200,000? _____

7. Which two states were admitted to the Union in 1959? _____

8. Who was the youngest man ever to become president of the United States? _____

   _____

9. What is the saltiest body of water in the world? _____

10. Which state is called the "mother of presidents" because eight United States presidents were born there? _____

Name _____

State Trivia

1. Which state is the smallest? _____

2. Name the steel state of the South. _____

3. Name the state that contains Hoover Dam, one of the world's highest dams, which supplies

   water and electric power to three western states. _____

4. Name the state in whose largest city more automobiles are made than in any other city

   in the world. _____

5. Which state was originally called the Sandwich Islands? _____

6. Which state touches more neighboring states than any other? _____

7. In which state were the first college and the first public school founded? _____

8. Which state's name is a combination of two French words meaning "green mountain"?

   _____

9. Which state is bounded on three sides by water and was the site of the first United States

   earth satellite launch? _____

10. Name the state that contains more than ten thousand lakes. _____

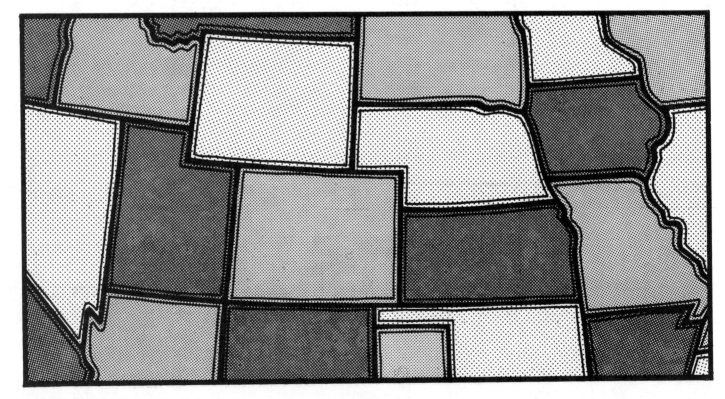

Name _____

Transportation

1. In China and Japan, people once rode in two-wheeled carts pulled by runners. What were these carts called? _____

2. In 1662, Blaise Pascal, a French scientist, devised the horse-drawn wagon that gave Paris the first public mass-transportation system. The English word *bus* is a shortened form of the name for this wagon. What was this wagon called? _____

3. What was the name of Robert Fulton's first commercial steamboat? _____

4. In what year was the first successful subway built in London? _____

5. Which German company built and flew the first jet airplane in 1939?_____

6. In 1954, the United States Navy launched the world's first atomic-powered ship. Name this vessel. _____

7. What is the name of the private corporation that was established by Congress in 1970 to operate most of the passenger trains in the United States? _____

8. Most of the river transportation in the United States is on the Mississippi River system. What seven rivers does this system include? _____

_____

9. In what city is John F. Kennedy International Airport located? _____

10. The largest passenger ship in the world is longer than three football fields and is 110 feet wide. Name this vessel. _____

Name _____

The Westward Movement

1. Which city in Virginia was the site of the first permanent English settlement in America?

    _____

2. Which American pioneer opened the Wilderness Road, one of the main routes across the Appalachian Mountains in the central region, thereby making possible the first settlement of Kentucky? _____

3. What was the main route used by pioneers to cross the Appalachian Mountains in the north?

    _____

4. What 1803 event opened a vast area west of the Mississippi River to American settlers?

    _____

5. Sent by President Thomas Jefferson to explore recently acquired lands, Meriwether Lewis and William Clark began their eighteen-month odyssey in St. Louis, Missouri, and ended it when they reached the Pacific Ocean at the mouth of what river? _____

6. Which canal was opened in 1825 to improve transportation westward? _____

7. Name the Mormon leader who brought his followers to the shores of the Great Salt Lake in 1847. _____

8. In what year did the discovery of gold inspire a rush to California? _____

9. The golden spike that connected Union Pacific tracks with Central Pacific tracks and symbolized the opening of the transcontinental railway was driven on May 10, 1869, at what place? _____

10. Which canal, built between 1904 and 1914, offered travelers going from the East Coast to the West Coast by ship an alternative to going "around the Horn"? _____

Name _____

The White House

1. What is the address of the White House? _____

   _____

2. Which architect designed the original White House in 1792? _____

3. What was the first official name given to the White House? _____

4. Who was the first president to live in the White House? _____

5. How many rooms are there in the White House? _____

6. How many rooms in the White House are ovals? _____

7. Which is the largest and most formal room in the White House? _____

8. Which room in the White House serves as the main reception room for guests of the

   president? _____

9. On what floor of the White House does the president live? _____

10. Which president had an indoor swimming pool added to the White House? _____

    _____

Name _____

Social Studies Search

The names of nineteen continents, countries, deserts, islands, mountains, parks, seas, states, and other things that are closely related to social studies are hidden in this box and listed below. Can you find all of them? Remember that these names may be written up, down, across, or diagonally and that they may read forward or backward.

```
A  B  C  A  C  I  R  E  M  A  D  E
M  A  U  N  A  L  O  A  O  H  I  O
A  R  A  G  H  A  L  T  U  I  J  E
I  A  K  L  I  I  Y  L  N  M  R  N
S  H  O  S  B  I  M  A  T  O  P  Q
S  A  A  E  S  A  P  S  M  A  P  S
U  S  R  L  F  H  U  H  C  L  M  N
R  T  A  R  A  O  S  P  K  A  Q  R
Y  N  I  W  S  U  T  U  I  S  V  W
D  C  A  X  R  Y  Z  A  N  K  B  C
A  I  D  D  N  E  G  E  L  A  E  F
I  D  E  A  D  S  E  A  E  R  I  E
G  E  T  I  M  E  S  O  Y  H  I  J
```

Africa	Erie	Ohio
Alaska	Hawaii	Olympus
America	legend	Rushmore
Asia	Liberty Island	Russia
atlas	maps	Sahara
Dead Sea	Mauna Loa	Yosemite
	Mount McKinley	

AMERICA HAWAII ERIE YOSEMITE
AFRICA OHIO MOUNT MC KINLEY
MAUNA LOA ASIA LIBERTY ISLAND

Answer Key

Page 5, Ancient Greece

1. Mount Olympus
2. Poseidon
3. 776 B.C.
4. Coroebus, a runner from the city of Elis
5. Milo of Croton
6. Herodotus
7. a fort
8. Doric, Ionic, and Corinthian
9. Ictinus
10. marble

Page 6, Geography

1. the Sahara
2. Asia
3. the Pacific Ocean
4. Australia
5. Sweden
6. Africa
7. Mount McKinley, which rises 20,320 feet above sea level
8. Asia
9. France
10. Canada

Page 7, Government

1. Sandra Day O'Connor
2. Leslie Lynch King, Jr.
3. San Clemente, California
4. Lyndon Johnson
5. Horatio
6. John Jay
7. Golda Meir
8. "Hail to the Chief"
9. Frances Perkins, an American social worker who served as secretary of labor under Franklin Roosevelt, from 1933 to 1945
10. Harry Truman

Page 8, Maps

1. cartographer
2. an atlas
3. legend
4. a bench mark
5. the equator
6. latitude
7. a relief map
8. a physical map
9. a political map
10. chart

Page 9, National Parks and Monuments

1. Wyoming
2. gypsum
3. Yosemite National Park
4. Utah
5. Mauna Loa
6. the Colorado River
7. Grand Teton National Park
8. the lily family
9. Rainbow Bridge
10. the General Sherman

Page 10, Places of Interest

1. Boulder Dam
2. seven
3. Big Ben (The bell was named for Sir Benjamin Hall, who was commissioner of works in 1856 when it was installed. This name is often given to the huge clock in the tower as well.)
4. the Paris Exposition of 1889
5. in Arlington National Cemetary, which lies in northern Virginia, across the Potomac River from Washington, D.C.
6. Old Faithful
7. Titusville, Pennsylvania
8. Liberty Island
9. in Houston, Texas
10. George Washington, Thomas Jefferson, Abraham Lincoln, and Theodore Roosevelt

Answer Key
(continued)

Page 11, Social Studies Potpourri
1. John Chapman
2. Howard Hughes
3. Yuri Gagarin
4. We
5. Cathay
6. Russia
7. Alaska and Hawaii
8. Theodore Roosevelt
9. the Dead Sea
10. Virginia

Page 12, State Trivia
1. Rhode Island
2. Alabama
3. Nevada
4. Michigan
5. Hawaii
6. Tennessee
7. Massachusetts
8. Vermont
9. Florida
10. Minnesota

Page 13, Transportation
1. jinrikishas
2. omnibus
3. the *Clermont*
4. 1863
5. the Heinkel Company
6. the U.S.S. *Nautilus*
7. Amtrak
8. the Illinois, Kanawha, Mississippi, Missouri, Monongahela, Ohio, and Tennessee rivers
9. New York City
10. the *Norway*

Page 14, The Westward Movement
1. Jamestown
2. Daniel Boone
3. the Mohawk Trail
4. the Louisiana Purchase
5. the Columbia River
6. the Erie Canal
7. Brigham Young
8. 1848
9. Promontory Point, Utah
10. the Panama Canal

Page 15, The White House
1. 1600 Pennsylvania Avenue, Washington, D.C., 20500
2. James Hoban
3. the President's House
4. John Adams
5. 132 rooms
6. three rooms
7. the East Room
8. the Blue Room
9. the second floor
10. Franklin Roosevelt

Page 16, Social Studies Search

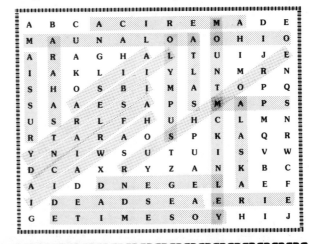

Name _____

Athletes

1. Who was the youngest tennis player ever to play at Wimbledon?_____

2. Which Romanian gymnast received seven gold medals and seven perfect scores of ten at the 1976 Summer Olympic Games in Montreal?_____

3. Which jockey was named Sportsman of the Year by *Sports Illustrated* at the age of seventeen?

   _____

4. Which boxer was nicknamed "the Brown Bomber"? _____

5. Which American swimmer was the first woman to swim across the English Channel, a distance of twenty-one miles? _____

6. What was George "Babe" Ruth's middle name? _____

7. Which athlete was the first American woman to win three gold medals in Olympic track and field competition? _____

8. Dick Button, Peggy Fleming, and Dorothy Hamill were all superstars in which sports event?

   _____

9. Which American Indian athlete won both the pentathlon and the decathlon in the 1912 Olympic Games and was called "the greatest athlete in the world" by the king of Sweden?

   _____

10. What name did boxer Cassius Clay later adopt? _____

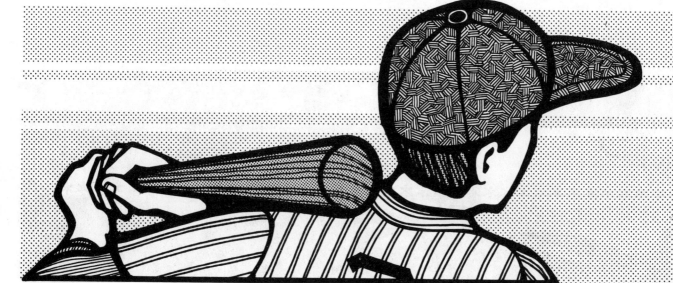

Name _____

Authors

1. What is the name of the eye doctor who wrote the Sherlock Holmes stories? _____
   _____

2. Which author wrote about herself and her three sisters in a popular book called *Little Women*?
   _____

3. Who wrote and published *Poor Richard's Almanac* each year for twenty-five years?
   _____

4. Washington Irving, author of "The Legend of Sleepy Hollow," was one of how many
   children? _____

5. What author wrote more than 156 fairy tales, including "The Emperor's New Clothes"
   and "The Ugly Duckling"?_____

6. What was the name of the ferocious white whale pursued by Captain Ahab in Herman
   Melville's novel? _____

7. What was Mark Twain's real name?_____

8. Who was the first American author to be awarded the Nobel prize for literature? ____
   _____

9. What is the title of the book written by Marjorie Kinnan Rawlings about a boy's love for
   his pet fawn? _____

10. What is the real name of the man who wrote *Alice's Adventures in Wonderland*?
    _____

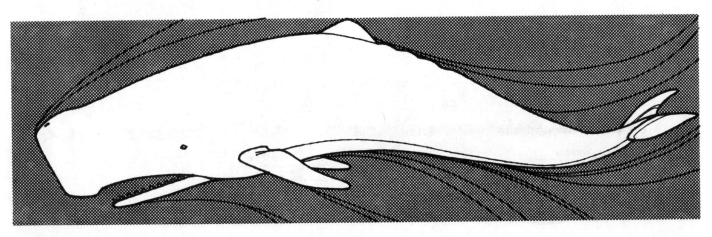

Name _____

Entertainment

1. In the movie entitled *The Wizard of Oz,* Dorothy, the Tin Man, the Scarecrow, and the Cowardly Lion must follow a particular route to reach the Emerald City of Oz. Name this route. _____

2. The movie called *Willy Wonka and the Chocolate Factory* was based on a book entitled *Charlie and the Chocolate Factory.* Who wrote this book? _____

3. What is the name of the addlepated character played by actor Peter Sellers in the movie called *The Pink Panther?* _____

4. Mary Poppins was nanny to what two children? _____

5. In a movie made in 1950, Elwood P. Dowd adopts a six-foot invisible rabbit as his friend. What is the name of the rabbit and the title of the movie? _____

6. In the Disney film entitled *Alice in Wonderland,* what character never has time to say hello or good-bye and frequently declares that he is late? _____

7. What three science fiction films pit Han Solo and a handful of rebels against Darth Vader and the evil forces of the Empire in a desperate struggle for galactic supremacy? _____

   _____

8. Who is commander of the starship *Enterprise* in the classic television series *Star Trek?*

   _____

9. What is the name of the family robot in the televison cartoon series called *The Jetsons?*

   _____

10. Who is Fred Flinstone's boss in the cartoon series? _____

Name _____

Explorers

1. Who was the first person to walk on the moon? _____

2. Which Portuguese sailor was the first to lead an expedition on a successful voyage around the world? _____

3. Which English explorer's ship was called the *Golden Hind*? _____

4. Who became the first man in space in 1961? _____

5. During the nineteenth century, a man known as Buffalo Bill rode for the pony express, scouted for the cavalry, served in the army, furnished buffalo meat for train construction crews, and ran a wild west show. What was this man's real name? _____

6. Name the famous pilot who made the first solo nonstop transatlantic flight, from Roosevelt Field in New York to Le Bourget Air Field in Paris, France, in May 1927. _____

7. What was the first name of the Spanish explorer Cortez? _____

8. How old was Alexander the Great when he died? _____

9. Which Portuguese explorer discovered a sea route to India by way of the Cape of Good Hope? _____

10. Name the American arctic explorer who reached the North Pole on April 6, 1909. _____

Name _____

Famous People Potpourri

1. Who was the first woman to graduate from a U.S. medical school? _____

2. Who is the author of the Winnie-the-Pooh stories? _____

3. Who invented the Frisbee? _____

4. What nickname was given to prison inmate Robert Stroud? _____

5. Who was the founder and first president of the American Red Cross? _____

6. Name the New York Jets quarterback who also acted on Broadway. _____

7. Who invented the process to make condensed milk? _____

8. What was Paul Revere's occupation? _____

9. Which United States astronaut became the third woman in space on June 18, 1983?

   _____

10. What was Billy the Kid's real name? _____

Name _____

Famous Quotes

1. Which Nobel prize winner said, "It is a great gift if one is permitted to work in science for his whole life"? _____

2. Who spoke the words, "Mr. Watson, come here, I want you," and what is their significance?

   _____

   _____

3. Name the person who said, "I know not what course others may take, but as for me, give me liberty or give me death"? _____

4. Who said, "It is rather for us to be here dedicated to the great task remaining before us . . . that government of the people, by the people, for the people, shall not perish from the earth"? _____

5. Which American naval officer responded to a British commander's call for surrender with the words, "I have not yet begun to fight"? _____

6. What United States president said, "I want to be the president who . . . helped to end war among the brothers of this earth"? _____

7. Which famous writer said, "The only way to have a friend is to be one"? _____

8. Name the American revolutionary hero whose last words were, "I only regret that I have but one life to lose for my country." _____

9. Name the young girl who wrote in her famous diary, "In spite of everything I still believe that people are really good at heart." _____

10. What famous civil rights leader said, "I have a dream that my four little children will one day live in a nation where they will not be judged by the color of their skin but by the content of their character"? _____

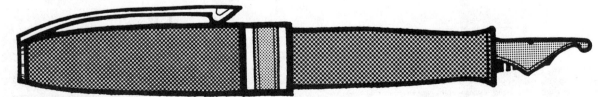

Name _____

Inventors

1. What woman scientist was the first person ever to win two Nobel prizes? _____

2. What famous black educator and agricultural scientist discovered more than three hundred uses for peanuts, soybeans, and sweet potatoes? _____

3. Who invented the cotton gin? _____

4. Whose theory of relativity changed the way people think about the universe? _____

    _____

5. Who invented the popular board game called Monopoly? _____

6. Who is credited with having invented the game of basketball? _____

7. Alexander Fleming discovered what important drug in 1928? _____

8. Who invented bifocal eyeglasses? _____

9. Which American inventor is credited with more than one thousand inventions, including both the electric light bulb and the phonograph? _____

10. Who invented Coca-Cola in Atlanta, Georgia, in 1886? _____

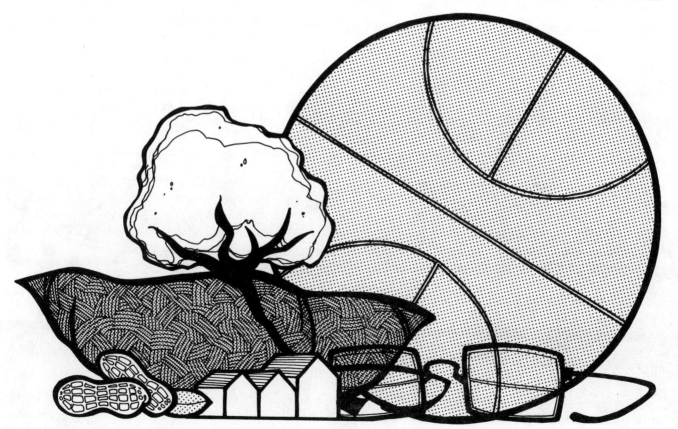

Name _____

Musicians

1. What blind black musician composed and recorded his first big hit, entitled "Fingertips," at the age of twelve? _____

2. What famous musical genius played the violin beautifully at the age of seven without ever having taken a lesson and wrote an opera when he was only twelve?_____

   _____

3. Who was the first woman conductor of the New York Metropolitan Opera Company?

   _____

4. Who is considered to be the "father of modern music"?_____

5. Which famous composer completed his famous Ninth Symphony after he had become totally deaf? _____

6. Who used jazz in an original symphonic work for piano and orchestra called *Rhapsody in Blue?* _____

7. Who became conductor of the Boston Pops after Arthur Fiedler?_____

8. What English rock group hit the top of the singles charts in 1964 with a record called "I Want to Hold Your Hand"? _____

9. What was singer Judy Garland's real name? _____

10. Music written by the composer known as the "king of ragtime" was used in a movie called *The Sting.* Name this composer. _____

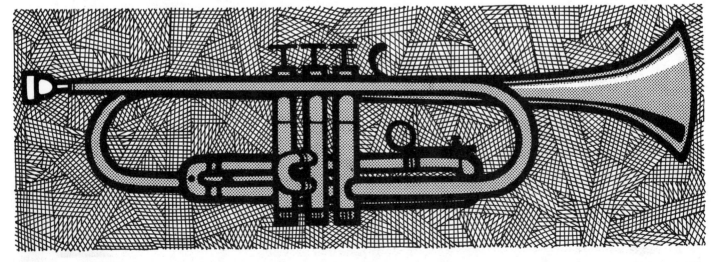

Name _____

Poets

1. Who is considered to have been America's first woman poet? _____

2. Poet Carl Sandburg wrote a detailed biography of what American president?_____

   _____

3. Name a poet who rarely capitalized letters and who used punctuation marks in unusual

   places and ways in his poems. _____

4. The poem "Annabel Lee" by Edgar Allan Poe was written in memory of whom? ____

   _____

5. What was poet William Bryant's middle name?_____

6. Which American poet wrote the poems "When Lilacs Last in the Dooryard Bloom'd" and

   "O Captain! My Captain!" in memory of Abraham Lincoln? _____

7. Name the Greek poet who wrote epics entitled the *Iliad* and the *Odyssey*. _____

8. A modern American poet wrote and illustrated a collection of humorous poems called

   A Light in the Attic, which set a record by remaining on the *New York Times* best-seller

   list for 112 weeks, longer than any other hardcover book in the fifty years that the list

   had been published. Name this poet. _____

9. What is the name of Hiawatha's wife in Henry Wadsworth Longfellow's poem entitled

   "The Song of Hiawatha"? _____

10. Who sailed away in a wooden shoe in Eugene Field's poem? _____

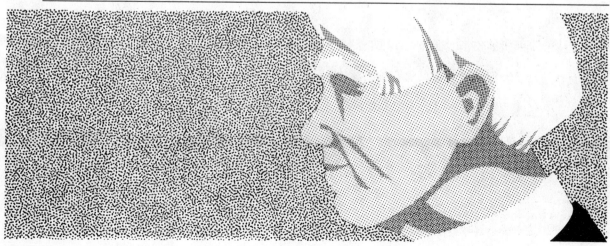

Name _____

Superheroes

1. The Joker, the Penguin, and the Riddler are enemies of what superhero? _____

2. What were the first names of Clark Kent's adoptive parents? _____

3. Dick Grayson is the real name of what superhero? _____

4. Scientist Dr. Robert Banner turns into what famous superperson? _____

5. Who is Popeye's hamburger-loving friend? _____

6. Where was Superman born? _____

7. What is Spiderman's real name? _____

8. Billy Batson was given superpowers by the wizard Shazam and became what famous superhero? _____

9. What superhero was hit by a lightning bolt and became the fastest man on earth?

    _____

10. What is the occupation of Hal Jordan, who is also known as the Green Lantern?

    _____

Name _____

United States Presidents

1. Who was the first president to live in the White House?_____

2. Which president served only one month and was the first to die in office?_____
   _____

3. Name the president who established the Peace Corps and also forced Russia to withdraw its missiles from Cuba. _____

4. Who was the first and only president to be married in the White House? _____
   _____

5. Which president organized the first U.S. Volunteer Cavalry, a group known as the "Rough Riders"? _____

6. Name the president who was a musician, an architect, and the inventor of the swivel chair.
   _____

7. Which president is known as the "Father of the Constitution"? _____

8. Which president bought the Louisiana Territory and, by doing so, doubled the size of the United States? _____

9. Who was president of the United States during the Great Depression and during World War II? _____

10. Who was the only man ever to serve first as president and then as chief justice?
    _____

Name _____

Famous People Search

The last names of fifteen famous people are hidden in this box and listed below. Can you find all of them? Remember that these names may be written up, down, across, or diagonally and that they may read forward or backward.

R	N	T	A	D	A	M	S	G	R
L	I	O	T	A	F	T	B	O	E
L	G	D	C	O	N	C	O	E	I
E	U	E	E	I	C	S	N	N	N
W	B	R	T	B	E	L	L	L	S
K	H	S	A	V	O	Y	A	I	T
C	U	I	E	C	D	C	O	M	E
A	G	L	N	O	T	R	A	B	I
L	T	I	C	Y	R	A	E	P	N
B	L	I	N	D	B	E	R	G	H

Adams	Blackwell	Milne
Alcott	Cody	Peary
Austin	Einstein	Ride
Barton	Lincoln	Roosevelt
Bell	Lindbergh	Taft

BLACKWELL MILNE AUSTIN
PEARY ROOSEVELT BELL
BARTON RIDE LINCOLN
LINDBERGH TAFT CODY
EINSTEIN ALCOTT

Answer Key

Page 19, Athletes
1. Tracy Austin
2. Nadia Comaneci
3. Steve Cauthen
4. Joe Louis
5. Gertrude Ederle
6. Herman
7. Wilma Rudolph
8. figure skating
9. Jim Thorpe
10. Muhammad Ali

Page 20, Authors
1. Arthur Conan Doyle
2. Louisa May Alcott
3. Benjamin Franklin
4. eleven
5. Hans Christian Andersen
6. Moby Dick
7. Samuel Clemens
8. Sinclair Lewis
9. *The Yearling*
10. Charles Dodgson

Page 21, Entertainment
1. the Yellow Brick Road
2. Roald Dahl
3. Inspector Jacques Clouseau
4. Jane and Michael Banks
5. Harvey
6. the White Rabbit
7. *Star Wars, The Empire Strikes Back,* and *Return of the Jedi*
8. Captain James Kirk
9. Rosey
10. Mr. Slate

Page 22, Explorers
1. Neil A. Armstrong
2. Ferdinand Magellan
3. Sir Francis Drake's
4. Yuri Gagarin
5. William Frederick Cody
6. Charles A. Lindbergh
7. Hernando
8. thirty-three years old
9. Vasco da Gama
10. Robert Peary

Page 23, Famous People Potpourri
1. Elizabeth Blackwell
2. A. A. Milne
3. Fred Morrison
4. the Birdman of Alcatraz
5. Clara Barton
6. Joe Namath
7. Gail Borden
8. silversmith
9. Sally K. Ride
10. William Bonney

Page 24, Famous Quotes
1. Albert Einstein
2. Alexander Graham Bell, inventor of the telephone, spoke these words to his assistant; and they were the first intelligible telephone message.
3. Patrick Henry
4. Abraham Lincoln
5. John Paul Jones
6. Lyndon Johnson
7. Ralph Waldo Emerson
8. Nathan Hale
9. Anne Frank
10. Martin Luther King, Jr.

Answer Key
(continued)

Page 25, Inventors
1. Marie Curie
2. George Washington Carver
3. Eli Whitney
4. Albert Einstein's
5. Charles B. Darrow
6. James Naismith
7. penicillin
8. Benjamin Franklin
9. Thomas Alva Edison
10. Dr. John S. Pemberton

Page 26, Musicians
1. Stevie Wonder
2. Wolfgang Amadeus Mozart
3. Sarah Caldwell
4. Johann Sebastian Bach
5. Ludwig van Beethoven
6. George Gershwin
7. John Williams
8. the Beatles
9. Frances Gumm
10. Scott Joplin

Page 27, Poets
1. Anne Dudley Bradstreet
2. Abraham Lincoln
3. e. e. cummings
4. Poe's wife
5. Cullen
6. Walt Whitman
7. Homer
8. Shel Silverstein
9. Minnehaha, which means "Laughing Water"
10. Wynken, Blynken, and Nod

Page 28, Superheroes
1. Batman
2. Jonathan and Martha
3. Robin, the Boy Wonder
4. the Incredible Hulk
5. J. Wellington Wimpy
6. on the planet Krypton
7. Peter Parker
8. Captain Marvel
9. Flash
10. test pilot

Page 29, United States Presidents
1. John Adams
2. William Henry Harrison
3. John F. Kennedy
4. Grover Cleveland
5. Theodore Roosevelt
6. Thomas Jefferson
7. James Madison
8. Thomas Jefferson
9. Franklin Delano Roosevelt
10. William Howard Taft

Page 30, Famous People Search

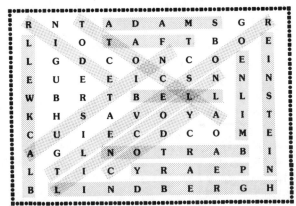